LEADERSHIP FOR
FINANCIAL FREEDOM

Michael Onalaja

Copyright © 2023

The rights of Michael Onalaja to be identified as the author of this work has been asserted by him in accordance with the copyright laws.

All rights reserved.

No part of this publication may be reproduced, stored in a retrieval system or transmitted in any form or by any means, electronic, mechanical, photocopying, recording or otherwise without the prior permission of the author or publisher.

Layout and Design by:
Heart2World Publishing
Ago Palace Way. Lagos
w. heart2worldpublishing.org
t. 09056183960
e. heart2worldpublishing@gmail.com

For information on distribution, translation or bulk sales, please contact:
Michael Onalaja
Phone: +234-909-596-6301
Email: Onalajamichael@gmail.com

DEDICATION

*For dreamers and doers, this book is for you.
To everyone wanting a better money story, let these words be your guide.*

Disclaimer

The information provided in this book is for informational purposes only.

The publisher and the author do not make any guarantee or other promise as to any results that may be obtained from using the content of this book. You should never make any investment decision without first consulting with your own financial advisor and conducting your own research and due diligence. To the maximum extent permitted by law, the publisher and the author disclaim any and all liability in the event any information, commentary, analysis, opinions, advice and/or recommendations contained in this book prove to be inaccurate, incomplete or unreliable, or result in any investment or other losses.

Content contained or made available through this book is not intended to and does not constitute legal advice or investment advice and no attorney-client relationship is formed. The publisher and the author are providing this book and its contents on an "as is" basis. Your use of the information in this book is at your own risk.

Book review

Sequel to his first book, 'Financial Freedom 101', Pastor Michael Onalaja in this masterpiece, 'Leadership for Financial Freedom', brings another compelling perspective to the subject of Financial Freedom by proving beyond all reasonable doubt that the duo, Leadership and Financial Freedom are intrinsically connected, viz, financial Success can most assuredly be achieved through selfless service to humanity.

On that note, Pastor Michael Onalaja generously lavishes the reader herein with his successful true life leadership experiences with his group of over twenty thousand adherents, based on leadership traits culled from the Life's Manual.

Additionally, Pastor Michael Onalaja addresses the pivotal roles that issues such as, love, gratitude and effective communication play on the subject-matter.

These and others make this unique book a compendium of information and exposition about Leadership and Financial Freedom for those who want to soar higher in the Financial Ecosystem.

I therefore heartily recommend that you read it, meditate on it, digest it and make it all your own.

Barrister (Mrs) Mercy Jackson

FOREWORD

I eagerly accepted the offer to write this foreword since I have seen the author's unwavering dedication to excellence, morality, and selfless accomplishments throughout the years. His idea of promoting improved managerial and leadership abilities, as well as upgrading and fostering individual performance potential, intrigues me.

Reading this book is a breeze!

This insightful work offers a comforting message of genuine hope to the wise, as it presents advice and real-world examples from renowned global leadership experts. It demonstrates that anyone can achieve success and long-term financial freedom by adhering to the vital codes of prosperity that are expertly packaged in this one-of-a-kind book.

As a discerning, soulful, and experienced leader, he upheld the truth of what he learned so far from trials and errors on his march to significance for the benefit of humanity. His writing style appeals to everyone who aspires to freedom and become a benefit to others, not just those in the leadership school but also to those in business and industry.

I have no doubt that each reader will obtain insightful practical knowledge that will enable them to transform hopes into reality and aspirations into manifestations.

'Wale Oyeniyi
New-World International Learning Solutions Ltd.
United Kingdom

Table of Content

Dedication   3
Book review   5
Foreword   7
Author's note   11

Chapter One:
    Financial Intelligence   17

Chapter Two
    Leadership   25

Chapter Three
    The Purpose of Leadership   33

Chapter Four
    Your Identity   39

Chapter Five
    The Making of a Leader   45

Chapter Six   57
    Turning your fear into financial freedom

Chapter Seven:
    The Magic of Actions   71

Chapter Eight   81
    The Leadership Traits for Financial Freedom

Chapter Nine
    The Core Value of Leaders   103

Chapter Ten
    Building Your Dream Team   109

Chapter Eleven
    The Ultimate Price: Sacrifice   123

Chapter Twelve
    The Power of Gratitude   133

Final words   *142*
About the author   *144*

Author's Note

If you want to make a lot of money, you need to be a good business person. Successful business people are often also great leaders. Take Bill Gates, for example; he is not just an entrepreneur but also a leader. For most businessmen and businesswomen, being a leader is key to using their skills and everything else in their work. If an entrepreneur does not understand leadership, he will not go far or be super successful.

Why?

Leadership is about managing people, while entrepreneurship is about managing resources, which includes people. Leadership focuses more on your people skills and ability to manage others, while entrepreneurship is simply managing all kinds of resources.

You cannot make money without thinking about leadership, and you cannot ignore entrepreneurship either. To build an organization, you need to be a great leader. To manage your organization's resources well and make a profit, you also need to be a great entrepreneur. These three things are closely connected; you cannot separate them.

Entrepreneurs who lack leadership skills usually fail because they cannot scale their ideas. Many entrepreneurs struggle or stay average because they do not master leadership. That is why it is interesting because combining them is like talking about the body and the spirit - one cannot function without the other.

This book, "Leadership for Financial Freedom," aims to make you realize that leadership is a crucial skill if you want to accumulate a lot of wealth. There is a difference between making some money and making a ton of it. Billionaires are different because they can scale things up. They see the big picture and make it happen. For example, Bill Gates wanted a computer in every home worldwide - that is scaling.

Steve Jobs sold iPhones globally; he had a global vision. Most billionaires become billionaires because they know how to scale. On the flip side, some people lack leadership abilities. They may have good ideas, but they stay small, serving only their local community. There is a gap between local and global success. Scaling means reaching billions of people, and for that, you need excellent leadership skills.

Many entrepreneurs have an average life because they lack leadership. Let us start with the story of McDonald's. Your organization can only grow as much as your leadership is effective.

In 1954, in the sunny town of San Bernardino, California, two brothers named Richard and Maurice McDonald were running a very successful restaurant – the first-ever McDonald's. They had a unique system that changed how fast food worked, making it quick, efficient, and consistent. People loved it, forming long lines to get a taste of this fast food magic.

However, their success was limited to their local area. The McDonald Brothers could not figure out how to take their thriving business to a global level. They were stuck in the idea that success only meant being popular in their hometown and couldn't imagine going beyond that.

On the flip side, a guy named Ray Kroc, who sold

milkshake machines, saw something big. When he visited the McDonald Brothers' restaurant, he noticed the long lines and efficient processes. It hit him – McDonald's could be more than just one restaurant; it could be a worldwide sensation.

Ray Kroc was a leader. He understood the potential and saw McDonald's as a global brand. The McDonald Brothers, on the other hand, could not wrap their heads around expanding so much. They hesitated and did not want to let go of control. Their lack of leadership skills became a big problem.

Ray Kroc did not wait. Seeing that the brothers could not take their creation global, he bought the rights to McDonald's and turned it into a corporation. He became the driving force behind McDonald's success worldwide.

Kroc's leadership was the reason McDonald's became a global icon. He had the vision, ambition, and skills to manage people and resources. His leadership made McDonald's grow not only in the United States but all around the world. In contrast, the McDonald Brothers' lack of leadership skills kept them limited to one place, and they lost control over what they created. The McDonald Brothers and Ray Kroc's story teaches us a big lesson about leadership in business. It shows that leadership skills are crucial for taking a business to new heights and achieving financial success.

1

FINANCIAL INTELLIGENCE

Chapter One

"It's not how much money you make, but how much money you keep, how hard it works for you, and how many generations you keep it for."
- Robert Kiyosaki

Your leadership affects your organizational growth, which, in turn, affects your financial growth. You cannot outgrow your mindset; what is inside shows outside.

In this book, we will explore leadership principles that can open the door to financial freedom. You will learn how to scale your ideas, businesses, and investments from local to global success. I believe that this book will not be completed without mentioning the importance of financial education in attainment of financial freedom.

Financial intelligence is the spirit while financial freedom is the body. Financial intelligence is like the cause while financial freedom is like the effect. Without proper financial education, it is almost impossible to achieve financial success in life.

If you want to have money, you must be willing to learn about money. You must get into the money game if you want to achieve financial freedom in life.

Whether or not anyone will become wealthy largely depends on his daily financial decisions. Poverty comes from poor thinking and poor financial decisions that people make in life. And that is as a result of lack of money management skills. So for you to attain financial freedom, you must learn how to achieve it.

For you to be financially free, you need to be financially intelligent. You must break free from some myths and embrace some facts.

1. *Poor People Work For Money:*
The program that was handed down to the lower class and the middle class by their parents is "Go to school and get a good grade so you can find a good job that will pay you well with good benefits." Most people follow this program given to them by their parents. So they live from paycheck to paycheck, running the rat race.

Many of the people who fall into this category live under serious financial stress rather than being financially free. The wealthy believe that money should work for them. They prefer to leverage money and people to get more and more money in life. Living with the program handed to you by your parents will lead you to more and more financial stress in life because that program is no longer working in this age and time.

We are in the Information Age and in this age, you have to be informed to be transformed. My mentor told me early in life that if I want to make money in life, I must learn how "not to work for money".

2. Rich People Chase After Things:
If you study the lifestyle of the middle class, you will see that they accumulate things. They like to buy the latest cars, the latest shoes, the latest wristwatches and so on. In fact, they love to buy things that are in vogue. They like to acquire designer-made bags, clothes, shoes, gadgets and what have you.

The people in this category believe that income plus debt equals wealth. They have all kinds of debts that they are servicing in their various places of work. They are always living on loans. More often that not, they accumulate liabilities. Most of them don't know the difference between assets and liabilities. They buy toys and bicycles for their children. They live to keep up with the Joneses, and with whatever is latest and in vogue. They don't know that the goal is not to look rich but to be rich.

Though the wealthy also have a luxury lifestyle, they buy it from the cashflow generated by their assets. The middle class live all their lives paying bills and running expenses on liabilities as a result of their poor financial decisions.

3. Wealthy People Know The Difference Between Assets And Liabilities While The Rich Chase After Things:

The wealthy chase after ideas and income-generating assets. They channel their money into income-generating assets that make them more and more money in life. Like one of my mentors said, the direction of your cashflow is everything in life. Many people are poor not because they don't have money but because they do not know how to manage money.

The understanding of the difference between assets

and liabilities helps them to use their money to acquire assets that produce enough passive income that fund the kind of lifestyle they desire.

The rich and the middle class buy luxury lifestyle from their loans and hard earned income. Wealthy people, on the other hand, buy luxury from income generated by their assets. For every penny they spend, they have put in place corresponding systems that replace it.

Wealthy people pursue ideas that make them become richer daily rather than accumulating liabilities for themselves. Wealthy people enjoy making more and more money than they enjoy spending. Someone said, "If you want to be wealthy, there's only one way to do it. It is spend less than you make, then for the remaining, multiply and accumulate it, you will get wealthy".

According to Robert Kiyosaki, an asset is anything that puts money into your pocket while a liability is anything that takes money out of your pocket. The bottom line is that while the rich chase after things that get them into more and more debt, the wealthy chase after ideas and income-generating assets that bring them more and more money.

The direction of your cashflow is everything. Money

mastery and money management is very fundamental to wealth accumulation. A wise man once said, "It is not what you make that matters but what you keep out of what you make and invest, is what will determine whether you will become rich or not". Prosperity comes from frugality. Money management is the mother of wealth creation.

4. The Money Tree:

I often hear people say that money does not grow on trees. My mentor told me it does, because money is a product of wood. The paper money is made from wood. However, what is considered as money trees in this context is cashflow. According to the book, *The Millionaire Fast Lane*, building and monetizing systems are the way to wealth. And these are considered to be the money trees:
- Rental system
- Software system
- Network system
- Information system
- Human resource system

You will never become wealthy until you create a system that can work without you; and a system is a repeatable process put in place that produces consistent results, and can work without you.

5. Financial Freedom Is Duplication:

Without duplication, you cannot have multiplication. No matter how good your products or ideas are, it would do you no good unless you distribute. In order to distribute, you have to duplicate or mass produce to reach millions of people.

For you to achieve financial freedom, you must learn to duplicate your ideas, systems, products or yourself. The law of wealth states that your financial freedom will be directly proportional to the value that you deliver to the marketplace. To make millions, you must be willing to serve millions of people. To make billions, are you willing to serve billions of people?

Money comes through two means, magnitude or amplitude. For instance, you either sell a product of $1,000 that has a 20% mark up to 100,000 people. The revenue would be $100,000,000. But your profit would be $20,000,000. Or you sell a product for $100,000,000 and make a 20% profit margin on it.

The financial intelligence discussed here are not exhaustive, there's always more.

LEADERSHIP

Chapter Two

> "A leader is one who knows the way, goes the way, and shows the way."
> - John C. Maxwell

Entrepreneurs who lack leadership might do well locally, but they'll struggle to grow and become massively successful. This story highlights that the growth and success of any organization are closely linked to the leadership skills of its leaders.

So, why is leadership so important, and what does it mean for entrepreneurs and those aiming for financial success? Let me share with you the story of John D. Rockefeller:

John D. Rockefeller was a big shot in the oil business a long time ago. His story can teach us a lot about how to lead and be successful.

JD Rockefeller was like a captain of a big ship in the world of oil. Back in the day, he had to decide how to move his oil around. The train companies had a lot of control, and they wanted things their way. But instead of giving in, Rockefeller decided to build pipelines. It was a bold move, like saying, "I'll do it my way!" This decision changed everything and showed how a leader can think differently and take charge.

Rockefeller didn't just sit in an office. He made sure everyone in his company thought about how to do things better. He believed that the way people think inside a company shows on the outside. Just like how you can't outgrow your mind, a company can't outgrow its way of thinking.

He led his team to be smart and efficient. It was like planting seeds for success. The company, called Standard Oil, grew and grew. It became the go-to for oil. This shows that good leadership is like good soil for a plant—it helps things grow.

Rockefeller knew that being smart with money was key. It wasn't just about making money; it was about understanding how money works. He believed that knowing about money is like having the power (spirit) and having money is like the result (body). Without knowing how money works, it's super hard to be successful.

He'd probably say, "If you want money, you gotta learn about it. Play the money game to win at financial freedom."

Every day, he made decisions that helped his company grow. He believed that becoming rich or poor depends a lot on what you do with your money every day. It's like a game—make good moves, and you win. Make bad ones, and you might lose. Poverty, he thought, comes from not thinking smart and making poor choices. That's because some people don't know how to handle money well.

So, a wise man once said, "To be free with money, you need to be smart about it. Break free from wrong ideas and embrace the right ones."

In simple words, Rockefeller's story is a big lesson in leadership. His choices and the way he led Standard Oil were like a guide for success. It's not just about having a big company; it's about leading with a smart mind.

So, what can we learn from JD Rockefeller? First, think differently. Don't just follow what others say. Second, make sure everyone in your team thinks smart too. It's like helping your plant (company) grow by giving it good soil (smart thinking). Lastly, understand the money game. If you want to win, you've got to learn how to play.

In the end, Rockefeller's story isn't just an old tale. It's like a message from the past saying, "Leadership is not just a title. It's about how you think and act to make things grow."

How can we apply his wisdom to becoming financially intelligent?

1. Think Smart:
Rockefeller lived like a superhero with money because he thought differently. You can do that too! When things are tough, don't give up. Instead, think about how you can make things better. A smart thinker finds solutions.

2. Be Money Smart:
Just like Rockefeller made his company work better, you can make your money work better for you. You just have to know where your money goes and make a plan. It's like being the boss of your money. Don't let money boss you around!

3. *Your Money, Your Rules:*

Rockefeller didn't follow what everyone else was doing. He made his own rules. You can do that with your money too. Decide what's important and spend your money on that. Be the boss of your choices!

4. *Plant Money Seeds:*

Rockefeller talked about planting seeds for success. For us, it means putting money where it can grow. Think about saving and investing. It's like planting seeds that grow into big trees. Your money can grow too!

5. *Break Free from Money Myths:*

Sometimes people say things about money that aren't true. You can be smart by asking questions and finding out what's real about money. Don't believe everything you hear! Read books, attend seminars, find a millionaire mentor to teach you as well.

6. *Learn About Money:*

If you want to be good with money, you need to know about it. It's like playing a game. Learn the rules, and you can win! Read books, watch videos, and ask questions. The more you know, the better you can play the money game.

7. *Play the Money Game:*

I see money as a game to be played and mastered. In

fact, my second book is titled "Winning The Money Game". You can play and win the game of money too!

Life is not only about having lots of money; it's about using what you have wisely. Try new things, take a few risks, and be part of the game. You might win big!

3

THE PURPOSE OF LEADERSHIP

Chapter Three

> "The function of leadership is to make ordinary people do extraordinary things."
> - Peter Drucker

Talking about leadership is like discussing the keys to financial success and starting your own business. To really get why leadership matters, let us dive into what it is all about and how it plays a big role in making money.

Remember the story about Ray Kroc and the McDonald Brothers? Well, that showed us how leadership can totally change the game.

Why is leadership so important?

Leadership is the art of showing, influencing, and motivating people to reach a common goal or dream. It is the set of skills that lets you manage and lead others really well.

Here are three big reasons why leadership matters:

1. Being Great Together:
Leadership is the way to achieve greatness, not just by doing well on your own but by helping others succeed too. While success is what you do by yourself, greatness is when you can get others to do amazing things. A great leader knows how to bring out the best in a team, making them achieve way more than they thought possible. Leadership is not just about you – it is about making a team stronger.

2. Making Your Ideas Big:
One of the main jobs of a leader is to help someone turn their idea or business into something huge. This means taking a local success and turning it into a big deal globally. Look at what Ray Kroc did with McDonald's – that is leadership at work. Without good leadership, your business might stay small and not reach its full potential.

3. Setting Up Smooth Operations:
Leadership is not just about telling people what to

do. It is also about creating systems, processes, and structures that make a business run really well. Good leaders know how to divide tasks and set up things so the business can run smoothly even when they're not around. By breaking down big tasks into smaller, manageable ones and putting the right people in charge, leaders make sure the business keeps growing and doing well.

Ray Kroc's taking over McDonald's shows all these things about leadership. He saw the chance to be great through others, expand McDonald's globally, and set up efficient systems for success in lots of places.

If you are on a journey to financial success and starting your own business, understanding leadership is a must. Without leadership skills, it is hard to make your ideas big, share the load, and set up things to run well. A lot of talented people struggle to reach their full potential because they do not work on their leadership skills.

Leadership is not just about growing a business; it is important in families, organizations, and communities. It is what keeps everything together in our world. Being a good leader is not limited to any one thing; it works everywhere and has a big impact.

Leadership is the way to be great, make your ideas big, and set up things to run smoothly – all crucial for finding financial success.

4

YOUR IDENTITY

Chapter Four

"To lead others, you must first lead yourself, understanding the depth of your own identity."
- Plato

On your journey to financial freedom through leadership, it is crucial to tackle the basic challenges that hold you back. The key to this pursuit is understanding and embracing your leadership identity.

Firstly, it is important to know that leadership is not a quality only a few people have. It is not a gift for the chosen ones; it is a trait in everyone. Some people wrongly think you are either born a leader or you are not, a belief that can hinder your path to financial freedom.

In reality, we all have leadership potential. If we are created in the image of God, the ultimate leader, then we too are leaders. Just as a lion gives birth to a lion, if we are God's children, we are born leaders. This idea is rooted in the belief that from the beginning, God instilled leadership qualities in us. When He made you in His image, He gave you His attributes. So, everyone is a leader at his core.

But being born with leadership potential and realizing it are different things. Some people, like an eagle raised among chickens, are held back by limiting beliefs and a lack of self-awareness. These beliefs can stop them from recognizing their true potential, leading them to live ordinary lives, unaware of their natural leadership abilities.

This is where identity comes into play. Before you can use leadership for financial freedom, you must acknowledge your identity as a leader. This is important because when people are facing challenges like addiction, crime, or other issues, they might not be aware of their leadership potential. Hearing a message of hope and transformation is an invitation to change, and this change starts with a shift in identity.

Changing your identity is crucial because it is the essential first step towards leadership. It is like saying, "I am now a leader." This shift sets the stage for behavioural change. Similar to the eagle that finally realizes its true nature and soars high, you need to recognize your potential as a leader. You must declare, "I am a leader" and repeat it until your subconscious internalizes this truth. Only then can you start leading effectively.

Your identity significantly influences your actions. What you believe about yourself affects how you behave. Just as a lion does not graze on grass because it knows it is a predator, knowing your identity as a leader shapes your actions and decisions. If you fail to define your identity, you will find yourself distracted and uncertain about your life's purpose.

So, the journey to financial freedom through leadership starts with understanding and embracing your identity. Once you define yourself as a leader, you will align your actions with this new self-perception. Your being dictates your doing. With a solid sense of identity, you can focus on the right activities that lead you to financial success.

Now, a significant challenge we face is that crucial components like financial intelligence, leadership, and entrepreneurship are not typically taught in schools and universities. These subjects are fundamental for success in every area of life, including financial freedom.

Financial intelligence, for example, is often overlooked in education. The art of managing money, making it grow, and securing your financial future is rarely emphasized in traditional schooling. Similarly, the concept of leadership is often ignored in universities. Many people leave school with degrees but lack the leadership skills they need for success.

Entrepreneurship is also frequently underrepresented in academic settings. Yet, it is a vital skill for creating financial freedom. The lack of education in these areas contributes significantly to the struggles people face in achieving financial success.

To bridge this educational gap and set you on the path to financial freedom, it's essential to acknowledge the significance of leadership. You must become a student in the school of leadership, just like in any other field. Embracing leadership as a core part of your identity is the first step to unlocking your potential and realizing your dreams of financial freedom.

5

THE MAKING OF
A LEADER

Chapter Five

"Leadership is the capacity to translate a vision into reality."
- Warren Bennis

On the journey to financial freedom, becoming a great leader is significant. Instead of just chasing profits, successful leaders prioritize a deeper sense of purpose. Purpose is like a guiding North Star—it is not just about making money, but about fulfilling a calling that comes from within. While a job is what you are paid to do, purpose is what you are born to do. Purpose is something deeper, rooted in your very being.

Leadership, the cause in the story of life, is closely connected to financial freedom—the desired effect. The strength of your leadership determines your financial success. Think of your leadership abilities as a lid, either holding you back or propelling you forward toward greater financial achievements. To achieve financial freedom, you need to consciously and intentionally develop your leadership skills.

Understanding the difference between purpose and vision is essential. Purpose comes from God and is the essence of your life. Vision, on the other hand, is the extent of life. Vision is a human creation that outlines your internal ambitions. Purpose is what you're created to do. While vision is how far you want to go in achieving it. Purpose is the cornerstone of your existence and it forms the foundation for leadership.

Without purpose, leadership lacks a solid ground. Your journey to financial freedom starts with understanding and prioritizing purpose and vision. Vision provides clarity on what to do and what not to do, keeping you focused.

This journey towards leadership, fueled by purpose and guided by vision, has the power to transform not only your life but also the lives of those around you. Remember, leadership is the cause, while financial freedom is the effect.

Things to understand for your leadership to find expression:

1. Prioritize Purpose Over Profit:
Great leaders focus on more than just making money—they prioritize serving a purpose beyond the bottom line. Purpose is eternal. While vision is internal. It guides your life's cause and effect. Your financial freedom is closely tied to your leadership abilities, so intentional personal leadership development is crucial.

2. Know your Identity with Purpose:
To be an effective leader and achieve financial freedom, you must understand your identity. Your identity shapes your actions and determines your activities. Without a clear identity, you might drift into mediocrity. Recognizing yourself as a leader transforms your behaviour, and intentionally shaping your identity aligns your actions with your goals.

3. Broken Focus:
A broken focus is often caused by distraction or a lack of concentration. It hinders many people from reaching their full potential. A common mistake

many people make is confusing ambition with vision. Ambition is self-focused, seeking personal recognition, fame, and power. Vision, on the other hand, is about helping others on their journey to success. Leadership, built on humility, arises from a desire to serve others.

4. Get rid of breadwinner mentality:
Many folks get stuck in the breadwinner's trap, and it's like putting your dreams on hold. Having a breadwinner's mentality means you see yourself as the provider, but sometimes, people end up giving what they don't have—draining their own life force. You can't help others if you're not okay first. It's like trying to share your sandwich when you're still hungry!

Life's like a puzzle, and managing it matters. If you're not successful, how can you help others succeed? You can't give what you don't have. Financial freedom is like a reward for being super disciplined with your money. Sadly, many folks let their dreams fade away because of this breadwinner's mindset.

Leadership is like planting flowers; it starts with loving yourself enough to succeed and achieve financial freedom. But to do that, you need to be a money maestro. It's like being the boss of your dollars and cents. If you're not there yet, don't pretend you are. Stop playing God in people's lives. Super successful folks give back when they've made it big. It's called being a superhero for society.

Accumulation comes before distribution. They give, but not in a way that hurts their own dreams. Real giving happens when it's time to give back to society. That's when they become philanthropists—fancy word for super generous people.

Successful money masters don't let emotions run the money show. They're more logical than emotional. Some folks let their feelings guide their wallets, and that's like trying to fill a leaky bucket with water. The manual of life says, "Only the strong keep the treasure." So, stop giving money you don't have. Save yourself first before you start playing hero for others.

The life manual advises: when you're strong, then make others strong. It's like giving someone a boost when they're climbing a ladder. Many miss the memo, and that's why they don't hit the jackpot in life. Getting rich is like playing a game with a leadership mindset. It's about loving your neighbor as much as yourself, not more.

Some give so much to others that they forget about their own dreams. If you want to grab financial freedom, kick that breadwinner's mentality out of your life. It's time to be your own hero first, then help others climb the success ladder with you.

5. Get rid of entitlement mentality: Ever heard of the entitlement mentality? It's like expecting others to run your life. But if you want to be financially free, you need a different mindset—a leadership mentality.

Lots of folks struggle because they think others are responsible for their life—government, bosses, even your best friend's cat. This kind of thinking can stop your dreams. If you want financial freedom, ditch this thinking pronto.

Entitlement mentality is like thinking someone else is driving your life. Nope, it's all you. You're the boss, not them. If you don't take charge now, you might end up just dragging along in life. The sooner you start steering, the better.

Financial freedom comes with a leadership mentality. It's not just saying, "I'm in charge." It's really being in charge. Taking the wheel and steering towards your dreams. The more you take charge, the more you grow. It's like growing muscles; you've got to lift the weights.

Your life is your responsibility. Not your boss, not your neighbors, and definitely not your cat's responsibility. You determine your worth. If you're not given the chance to be financially free, make your own chance. Successful money masters don't let others run their lives. They grab the steering wheel and navigate their own financial destiny.

They learn what they need to learn, and they put it into action. They're like the superheroes of their own stories. And guess what? You can be your own superhero too. You've got one life, so start now. Don't let others dictate your journey—grab that steering wheel and drive towards your dreams!

6. Don't have a victim mentality: Many people fail in life because of this mentality. Some people feel like life's always against them. They blame everything on external stuff—government, politicians, even the neighbor's dog. This kind of thinking makes it hard for them to take control of their lives. With this mindset, finding solutions to challenges is like trying to find a needle in a haystack.

People with the victim mentality believe everyone's out to get them—government, politicians, spouses, you name it. They let life happen to them instead of making things happen. It's like they're stuck in a negative movie, always saying, "Everyone hates me. Life's not fair." But financial freedom needs a different script.

Leadership mentality means seeing yourself as a victor, not a victim. It's about being a hero, not just surviving. If you don't drop the victim act, financial freedom will be like chasing a rainbow. People who started from tough spots have risen to rule their worlds. You can do the same.

Stop seeing yourself as a victim of circumstances. Your background doesn't decide where you go. No matter what, you can turn things around. You've got potential inside you—wake up! Life isn't fair to everyone, but many turned their financial destiny around.

To see big financial freedom, drop the victim mentality. It's a roadblock to your success. Instead of waiting for people to do stuff for you, think about how you can help others. Be on the giving side, not just the receiving side. You're a light in this world; go shine and make a difference in others' lives. Develop a leadership mentality, and watch yourself win and achieve financial freedom! You're not a victim of life; you're the hero of your story. Time to take charge!

7. Embrace the responsibility mentality: the leadership mentality that guarantees financial freedom, requires responsibility mentality. Responsibility is the cost and the hallmark of leadership. Responsibility means, response-ability. It also means a sense of accountability.

Many people run away from taking responsibility in life, but that's contrary to leadership game. Great leaders assume more and more responsibilities to climb up in life. Responsibility mentality is a state of mind that always calls for accountability. Responsibility mentality in a leader, makes him know that necessity is laid upon him to create solutions for himself and for the people in general.

Many people who have responsibility mentality are problem solvers. They're very reliable people when it comes to their area of work. They operate a high level work ethics. They're always reliable and dependable. People with great sense of responsibility are always in high demand in our society. You must resolve to step up and begin to take responsibility for your life, if you want to achieve financial freedom in your life. You have to start now because nobody will help you to do that. Responsibility is a very good character trait that a leader must possess in his life. Leaders who possess this attribute are usually high flyers in our society at large. Start taking more and more responsibility in your life right now. The best time to plant a tree was 20 years ago. But the second best time is now.

TURNING YOUR FEARS INTO FINANCIAL FREEDOM

Chapter Six

Money is a tool in the hands of the wise; it builds bridges, not walls."
- Mike Onalaja

Not too long ago, a female reporter found herself in the midst of a conversation with a highly successful man. In pursuit of insights into the secret of success, she posed a fundamental question, "What is it that makes successful people successful in life?" The response she received was profound, the successful man said, "Success comes from the ability to make fast decisions." Intrigued, the reporter delved deeper, inquiring about the method to acquire the skill of making fast decisions. The answer she received was both enlightening and unconventional: "You learn to make fast decisions by being willing to make the wrong ones."

This seemingly contradictory standpoint was presented as the gateway to prosperity. It implied that welcoming the fear of failure is a necessary step towards achieving financial freedom in life. In essence, financial freedom is not a result of avoiding mistakes, but rather a product of transforming every decision, even the flawed ones, into opportunities for growth and financial freedom.

1. The Success Cycle: Redefined

Success, according to renowned author, John Maxwell, follows a cycle of self-improvement and organizational growth. This cycle comprises five fundamental steps:

I. Make good and fast decisions: Decision-making serves as the initial step in your journey to financial freedom. Act with intention and pace.

II. *Fail:* Do not dread failure; instead, embrace it as an invaluable learning opportunity. Understand that even a "wrong" decision might be a step in the right direction.

III. *Learn:* Each decision, regardless of its immediate outcome, contributes to your knowledge and personal development.

IV. *Improve:* With lessons learned from your experiences, strive for continuous improvement.

V. *Repeat:* The cycle perpetuates, reinforcing your path towards financial freedom.

2. Make good and fast decisions:

The art of making good and fast decisions is a proactive approach to decision-making that hinges on the belief that "If it's not the thing, it's the thing that will lead to the thing." Contrary to the fear of making mistakes, making swift and informed decisions is the foundation of success. Hesitation and indecision can significantly hinder progress. To succeed, it is essential to cultivate the habit of making quick, well-founded decisions, a valuable skill highly sought after in society.

It is not just about making good decisions; it is about making them swiftly. The premise here is to believe that even if the decision doesn't lead directly to the desired outcome or immediate financial freedom, it may still be a step in the right direction. Sometimes, what initially appears as a negative outcome may, in fact, be a positive one. The key is to maintain a perspective of forward momentum and embrace the learning that stems from each decision. Every choice contributes toward your financial freedom.

3. All things work together for your good.

An underlying principle to remember is that "all things work together for your good." Life unfolds in a web of interconnected events, both positive and negative, all contributing to your personal growth. To achieve financial freedom, you must trust that, ultimately, everything will align in your favour.

4. Overcoming the Fear of Failure

Fear of failure is a challenging hurdle on the path to financial freedom. To overcome this fear, you must act as if there are no limits to your abilities and firmly believe that success is already within reach. This perspective fosters the belief in your capacity to face challenges without succumbing to the paralyzing fear of failure. Visualizing your goals as already accomplished motivates the pursuit of financial freedom.

5. The Power of Faith

Believing that "With God, nothing is impossible"

instils a strong faith in God. This belief grants you hope, even in situations that seem impossible. It is an understanding that there is a source of strength and possibility beyond our abilities, influencing the path to financial freedom.

6. The Need for Speed: Success Loves Swift Decision-Making

Success is often closely linked to speed. Being decisive and making prompt decisions significantly impacts your ability to succeed. Hesitation and indecision can hinder your progress, making the skill of quick and sound decision-making highly valuable, leading to favourable outcomes.

7. Your Life as a Cumulative Result of Decisions

Understanding that your life's current state is the cumulative result of every choice and decision made until this point is important. The more decisions you make towards your financial freedom, the more successful you'll get. Both small and big decisions have shaped your present circumstances. Active decision-making is fundamental to achieving financial freedom.

OVERCOMING THE FEAR OF FAILURE

Procrastination is the bane of progress, but when one is paralyzed by the fear of failure, how can financial freedom be achieved? Actions are the cure for procrastination. Fear can be a powerful ally when harnessed effectively. You can actually turn your fear into financial freedom. Let us dive in and find out some good side of fear. There is treasure in darkness. There is financial freedom in fear if used positively and to your advantage.

FACE YOUR FEAR

Much like an eagle soaring to greater heights by confronting the storm, fear can serve as the leverage that propels successful individuals toward financial freedom. Rather than shying away from fear, many successful people boldly embrace it. Contrary to conventional wisdom, they move in the direction of their fear, recognizing that true growth and remarkable achievements lie beyond their comfort zones.

Successful individuals are masters of their emotions and fears, which is a key distinction between them and those who struggle to achieve financial success. Many individuals find it difficult to part with their hard-earned money, driven by an emotional attachment to their money and fear of failure. However, the understanding that fear guides you toward your growth path, reveals that the richest rewards often await on the other side of fear.

Success and substantial achievements are often situated on the other side of fear. As one wise individual once noted, "Every worthwhile achievement I've ever had scared me at first." Financial freedom is not achieved by avoiding fear but by managing and harnessing it effectively. When your life and business are running smoothly, it is a clue that you're not growing. Fear, when used correctly, becomes the compass pointing the way toward growth. The issue is not the presence of fear, but rather the direction in which you choose to take in relation to it.

Consider this: How often have you experienced genuine success without confronting any fear? Reflecting on your life, you will likely find that your most significant achievements occurred after facing and overcoming fear.

CONQUERING FEAR

1. Fear is Universal: It is essential to recognize that everyone experiences fear. What distinguishes us is how we respond to it. Some people allow fear to paralyze them, preventing them from taking risks or pursuing their goals, leading to unfulfilled potential. Others, however, use fear as a motivator, channelling it into positive energy and determination. This approach not only helps you achieve personal growth but also drives business growth and remarkable accomplishments.

2. Befriend Your Fear: Successful people do not turn away from fear; they embrace it. Instead of avoiding or ignoring fear, acknowledge it and leverage it to your advantage. Rather than allowing fear to hinder your progress, convert it into a trigger for action and growth.

3. Confronting Fear Leads to Growth: Personal growth often transpires when you confront your fears. Stepping out of your comfort zone and facing discomfort provides opportunities for learning and growth. Embracing your fears allows you to develop new skills, gain confidence, and expand your comfort zone, an ongoing process that extends throughout life.

4. *Push Beyond Your Comfort Zone for Growth:* Personal growth is most evident when you venture beyond your comfort zone. Confronting and conquering the fear of failure and limitations opens doors to new possibilities and financial freedom that may have seemed impossible in the past.

5. *Without friction, there is no progress:* You must understand that encountering challenges or obstacles is a necessary part of making progress or achieving financial success in life. When things are running smoothly, there is less motivation to improve your life. The process of overcoming friction leads to growth, learning and ultimately financial progress in life. Frederick Douglas said, "If there is no struggle, there is no progress " So facing challenges is a fundamental part of achieving financial success and moving forward in any area of life.

THE FIGHT-OR-FLIGHT DILEMMA

1. Response to Life's Challenges: It is not what happens to you in life that matters, but how you respond to it. The fear of failure can often stem from anticipating the worst rather than the best. It is a testament to the power of your thoughts. Your thoughts shape your reality, and mastering your thoughts can make you the master of your life. As the adage goes, "As a man thinks in his heart, so is he."

It simply means a man becomes his thoughts. He acts according to his thought or he is a product of his thought. The same life's manual also advises, it says, be careful how you think, because your thoughts make you the person that you become. Know that your thought is a form. Once you form your thoughts, they form your life. The people who master their thoughts, end up becoming the masters of their lives.

Most highly successful people create their thoughts, a habit that makes them so successful in the world. Know that thoughts become things. If you can control the thoughts in your mind. You can control the things in your life. Your dominant thoughts are what you reproduce in your life. I said reproduced because the world was created twice: it was first a thought, then a thing.

2. *Embrace the Struggle:* If you find yourself feeling fearful and struggling, give yourself that gentle push forward. Struggles and challenges are the crucibles of growth. Without struggle, there is no growth. Taking proactive steps, even in the face of fear, is a testament to your self-motivation and determination on the path to financial freedom.

3. *Understanding Fear:* Fear is a natural response, often indicating that something terrible might happen. It is a signal from your subconscious mind, designed to keep you in your comfort zone and prevent you from taking action. You have a choice in how you respond to fear: either face it head-on (fight) or avoid it (flight).

4. *Harnessing Fear for Financial Success:* Fear can be a driving force, propelling you toward a new level of financial success. When used correctly, fear can become a stepping stone to financial freedom, serving a valuable purpose in your life.

Turning your fears into financial freedom is a multi-faceted journey that involves embracing decision-making, conquering the fear of failure, and leveraging the power of fear as a guiding force.

Success lies not in avoiding fear, but in using it as a catalyst for growth and financial success. It is about making swift decisions, trusting the process, and understanding that challenges are an integral part of progress. When fear is harnessed and wielded effectively, it becomes a bridge to financial freedom and personal fulfilment.

7
THE MAGIC OF ACTION

Chapter Seven

> "Magic is not in the words we speak but in the actions that bring them to life."
> - Mike Onalaja

In the world of leadership and financial freedom, there is a profound truth that separates the successful from the rest. It is a simple, yet incredibly powerful concept: action is everything. If you look at those who have failed in their professions or endeavours, more often than not, it's because they didn't take action. Fear of failure often holds people back, paralyzing them and preventing them from moving forward. But here is the secret – fear of failure breeds procrastination, while action slays procrastination. Successful people have mastered the art of execution, and that is why they consistently achieve remarkable results.

Your journey to financial freedom is intricately linked to your ability to develop your leadership skills, particularly when no one is watching. What do you do when you are alone, when there is no one there to motivate or guide you? True leaders are perpetual learners, and they understand that learning doesn't stop at a certain hour. It is a continuous process, a habit, an attitude. They learn as they go, using every spare moment to enhance their knowledge and skills. There's no idle time and no downtime in a leader's life. They roll up their sleeves and put in the work, recognizing that results only come through diligence, commitment, dedication, and unwavering focus.

Execution is the missing link that separates those who succeed from those who do not. Until you become a master of execution, until you can take action despite your fears, your leadership journey will remain incomplete, and financial freedom will remain a distant dream. You see, many people mistakenly believe that wisdom is synonymous with information. In reality, knowledge is merely information; wisdom is execution. You can amass all the information in the world and still fail miserably if you do not turn that knowledge into action. It is not your intentions that produce results; it is your actions.

The magic that propels the world's great achievers, the top 1%, is the realization that action is the bridge between their dreams and their reality. It is the bridge between where they are and where they want to be. To achieve financial freedom, you must take consistent and persistent action. Leaders understand that their work is their life, and their life is their work. They know that results come from taking action, not just passing time.

Leaders do not measure their success by mere activities; they focus on accomplishments. Many people confuse motion with action, thinking that they're making progress when they are just moving in circles. The true secret to success lies in consistent action. This is where the magic happens. Those who consistently take action stand strong in the face of life's challenges. They are well-grounded, well-established, and more successful because their game is the game of action. The game of great achievers is built upon a foundation of constant and consistent action.

If you aspire to stand out and excel in your leadership journey, you must embrace constant action. This is the game that separates the 1% from the rest. It is the only producer of results, and great leaders understand this truth. They do not waste their time on trivial matters. They focus on what truly matters, and what truly produces results.

Little minds are preoccupied with trivialities, while great minds sweat the big stuff. They dream big and set their sights on ambitious goals. They make their dreams so big that they grow into them. Some may say, "Bite only what you can chew," but great leaders understand that the path to success is quite the opposite. They bite more than they can chew, knowing that this is how they attract divine assistance.

By reaching for dreams that surpass their capabilities, they beckon the help of a higher power to carry the load. Your dreams should always be bigger than your current size because that is when you will attract divine intervention to reach your destination.

Great leaders understand that the rule of engagement

in their journey is results. They dream big and think big because their focus is on nothing less than achieving results. There is real magic in action, and you can verify this for yourself by exploring the importance of taking action.

Taking consistent action propels your intentions into motion, moving you closer to your goals and desired results. Action is the driver of progress, helping you make steady headway toward your objectives. When you embrace constant action, you also invite constant growth and development into your life, momentum becomes your closest ally. Leaders understand that momentum is their friend. They do not wait for things to happen; they make things happen. They want to see constant progress, activity, and results. Their energy is always high, and they are eager to roll up their sleeves and put in the work.

One of the tremendous advantages of taking action is the boost it gives to your confidence. Imagine waking up in the morning with a to-do list and completing the first task. The effect is astonishing; it raises your self-esteem, improves your self-confidence, and ignites a can-do spirit within you. You start seeing yourself as a superstar, as a champion. The more tasks you conquer, the more confident you become.

Happiness, for leaders, stems from winning. Each achievement, no matter how small, is a victory. Success is defined as the constant and consistent achievement of predetermined goals. Therefore, every time you tick off a goal, you can celebrate your success. You do not need to wait for external validation to consider yourself successful; you become a winner with each goal you accomplish.

By taking on more responsibility and confronting challenges daily, leaders increase their self-esteem and self-confidence. Every hurdle they overcome becomes a source of motivation. They begin to see that they can conquer anything that comes their way. Constant action keeps them motivated, their self-esteem high, and their enthusiasm unwavering.

Another remarkable advantage of constant action is that it opens doors to constant opportunities. When you are consistently taking action, opportunities flow to you effortlessly. Action leads to unexpected opportunities, and you must be someone who loves taking action to reap these benefits.

By embracing constant action, you expose yourself to new experiences, connect with new people, and seize new opportunities. The more you act, the more you invite these opportunities into your life.

As a leader, you must be a role model for your team. Your actions speak louder than your words. Leadership is not about giving instructions; it is about demonstrating through your actions. People do not do what you tell them to do; they do what they see you do. To be an effective leader, you must lead by example.

Your actions inspire and motivate your team. You are the driving force behind their dedication and determination. By taking action consistently, you become an inspiration to those around you, igniting their desire to take action and achieve greatness.

Taking action is not just about having intentions; it is about turning those intentions into inventions. Your constant actions are a powerful testament to the world that you're not merely dreaming but actively working towards your goals. Action is the magic that transforms your desires into tangible results.

The magic of taking action cannot be overstated. It triggers progress, builds momentum, boosts confidence, opens doors to opportunities, and inspires others. As a leader on the path to financial freedom, constant action is your lamp. Remember, success is the constant and consistent achievement of predetermined goals, and can only be reached through persistent action.

The magic lies in taking action. Start doing.

8

THE LEADERSHIP TRAITS
FOR FINANCIAL FREEDOM

Chapter Eight

"The function of leadership is to produce more leaders, not more followers."
- Ralph Nader

In my journey to explore the connection between leadership and financial freedom, I have uncovered that these two aspects of life are deeply intertwined. The more you enhance your leadership abilities, the more you can expand your horizons in terms of financial success. It is not just a matter of a few isolated principles; it is a comprehensive package that we need to dig into.

The bedrock of financial success lies in the domain of leadership. It is not a mere coincidence that those who excel as leaders tend to enjoy more significant financial accomplishments. To understand this better, let us delve into the relationship between leadership competence and organizational growth.

Imagine your leadership competence as the engine that propels your organization forward. The degree of your leadership ability becomes the determining factor for the extent of your organizational growth. If you possess strong leadership skills, your organization is more likely to thrive and expand. On the other hand, if you lack leadership, it can become a limiting factor that hampers your organization's potential.

Think of your financial success as the sum of your organization's growth and your achievements. Your leadership prowess directly influences your organization's growth, and in turn, your financial success. To put it simply, your leadership abilities dictate the size of your financial success. The better leader you become, the greater your financial achievements can be. It is a symbiotic relationship; one depends on the other. Therefore, you must acknowledge that leadership is not a side note in the quest for financial freedom. It is the very essence of it.

THE COMPLETE LEADERSHIP PACKAGE

Now, you might wonder what specific leadership traits you need to take on to pave the way for financial freedom. The answer is clear - all of them. Leadership is not a pick-and-choose scenario. It is about mastering the complete package.

When a bricklayer is constructing a building, each pillar, beam, and brick plays a crucial role in supporting the structure. The absence of any one element can weaken the entire edifice. Similarly, in the world of leadership, every principle is essential to build a strong foundation for financial success.

Remember, there are good leaders, and then there are great leaders. The distinction lies in their grasp of these traits and their ability to put them into action.

1. VISION

One of the cornerstones of leadership is having a clear vision. A vision is like a lamp that guides your organization and your financial endeavours. It is the blueprint of where you want to go, what you want to achieve, and the impact you want to make.

A leader with a vision can see beyond the immediate

challenges and setbacks. They can inspire others to follow their path because they can articulate a compelling picture of the future. This vision acts as a powerful motivator for everyone involved, driving them to work towards a common goal. There can be a vision without a leader. But there can never be a leader without a vision. Vision is one of the hallmarks of leadership. Vision is an indispensable quality of a leader.

Vision is the foundation of effective leadership. A leader must be able to see beyond the present, to envision a future that others can not. Visionaries have a knack for seeing the end from the beginning, even before they take their first steps. This unique ability to see beyond the horizon is what sets them apart.

For those seeking financial freedom, a clear vision is equally important. It helps you define what financial freedom means to you. It could be early retirement, financial security, or the ability to pursue your passions without monetary constraints. Without a vision, it's challenging to navigate your financial journey, much like sailing without a destination in mind. Not having money, is like sailing without a compass.

Incorporate the leadership principle of vision into your financial planning. Picture your ideal financial future, set clear goals, and create a roadmap to get there. Your vision will act as a lamp, keeping you on track even when the seas get rough.

If your mind hasn't been there, your feet can hardly get there. Your vision not only needs to be big but also needs to be crystal clear. Having a vision is one thing, but the ability to communicate and paint that picture vividly is equally crucial. To attract followers, you must make your vision so compelling that people can't help but want to be a part of it. People always want to be part of something bigger than themselves.

2. COMMUNICATION

Vision alone is not enough; it needs effective communication to make it a reality. Effective leadership is not just about having a vision; it is about communicating that vision to your team and stakeholders. Communication is the glue that holds leadership together. It ensures that everyone is on the same page, working towards the same goals.

You must be a persuasive and engaging communicator. A visionary leader can inspire hope and paint a brighter future, even when times are tough. Leaders are "dealers in hope."

Great communication skills allow you to express your vision clearly, ensuring that others can understand and connect with it. People should feel emotionally invested in your vision, knowing that you can help them achieve their dreams because you've been where they are now.

You need to communicate your financial plans, goals, and strategies to those who are impacted by them. Whether it is your spouse, business partners, or financial advisors, effective communication ensures that everyone understands and aligns with your vision.

Communication is crucial in networking and building relationships. It is through communication that you can forge partnerships, seek advice, and explore investment opportunities. Great leaders and financially successful individuals are exceptional communicators.

3. ADAPTABILITY

The world is in a constant state of change, and leaders must adapt to these shifts. Adaptability is the ability to adjust your strategies, plans, and mindset to the evolving circumstances. It's about staying agile and responsive, even in the face of uncertainty.

Leaders are not rigid; they are adaptable. They embrace change and are flexible in the face of challenges. They are not confined to a single way of doing things. Instead, they try various approaches and stick with what works.

They navigate uncertainty with ease, assess alternatives, and choose the best course of action. Leaders do not let challenges keep them grounded; they keep moving forward.

Adaptability is equally important. The financial landscape is always shifting - markets fluctuate, new technologies emerge, and economic conditions change. If you are rigid in your financial approach, you risk being left behind.

Adaptable leaders not only survive but thrive in

changing environments. Similarly, those who can adapt to evolving financial situations are more likely to secure and sustain their financial freedom.

4. EMPOWERMENT

Great leaders do not just focus on their personal success; they empower others to achieve greatness. Empowerment is the process of delegating responsibilities, providing resources, and creating an environment where others can excel.

Leaders are inspirational figures. They motivate and inspire those around them. They instil a sense of purpose and enthusiasm in their team. Their energy and optimism are infectious, making people willingly tackle challenging tasks.

Empowerment means sharing knowledge, resources, and opportunities with those around you. It could be mentoring a colleague, guiding a family member in financial planning, or investing in initiatives that uplift communities. Empowerment not only creates a positive impact on others but also enhances your financial freedom journey.

When you empower others, you create a network of support and collaboration, which can lead to new financial opportunities and partnerships. Remember, financial freedom is not a solo endeavour; it is creating a fulfilling life for yourself and those you touch along the way.

5. RESILIENCE
Resilience is the ability to bounce back from setbacks, adversity, and failures. Great leaders understand that challenges are a part of any journey, and they use these setbacks as stepping stones to success.

Leaders do not give up; they face obstacles with unwavering determination and maintain a positive outlook. Success is the ability to move from failure to failure without losing enthusiasm, according to Wilson Churchill.

In the pursuit of financial freedom, you will encounter roadblocks, financial setbacks, and unexpected challenges. Resilience is your armour in these moments. It enables you to stay committed to your goals and maintain your financial course, even when things get tough.

Embrace the leadership principle of resilience by viewing failures as opportunities to learn and grow. It is through these experiences that you become stronger and more prepared for the road ahead. Financial freedom is often a result of enduring hardships and emerging from them with valuable lessons.

6. INTEGRITY

Integrity is the bedrock of leadership. It is the quality of being honest and having strong moral principles. Leaders who lead with integrity inspire trust and respect among their followers. It means doing what is right when others are watching and doing what is right even when no one is watching.

Integrity is a core trait of a great leader. It's not limited to honesty; it encompasses your entire character. Leaders with integrity are not only honest but also ethical, with strong moral principles. They are consistent in their actions and hold themselves accountable.

Leaders with integrity do not procrastinate. They take responsibility and act with values and principles, even in challenging situations. People trust leaders with integrity because they know they will deliver on their promises. Integrity also has to do with the ability to always keep to your promises. When you started up, you promised yourself that you were going to make it. If you can't fulfil the promise you made to yourself. How can you even fulfil the promise you made to others?

For financial freedom, integrity is non-negotiable. It means managing your finances honestly, paying your debts, and fulfilling your financial commitments. It also involves ethical investing and making financial decisions that align with your values. Integrity equals commitment.

Integrity in leadership and financial dealings builds a reputation that opens doors to opportunities and partnerships. It's an asset that can't be measured in monetary terms but plays a significant role in your financial journey.

7. INNOVATION
Innovation is the ability to think creatively and find new solutions to existing problems. Great leaders

are often innovative thinkers who can adapt to changing circumstances by introducing new ideas and approaches.

When it comes to financial freedom, innovation is essential. It means exploring new investment strategies, seeking out unconventional opportunities, and staying ahead of financial trends. Innovation can lead to financial breakthroughs that set you apart from the crowd.

By adopting the leadership principle of innovation, you can create financial strategies that are both unique and effective. It's about thinking outside the box and embracing change rather than fearing it.

8. ACCOUNTABILITY

Accountability is the obligation to take responsibility for one's actions and decisions. Great leaders hold themselves accountable for their choices and performance, setting an example for those they lead.

Leaders take accountability seriously. They do not just take responsibility; they embrace it and assume more responsibility as they progress. They understand that solving one problem immediately leads to a more complex one. Leaders see problems as stepping stones to success.

Accountability means taking ownership of your financial decisions and their consequences. It involves setting and tracking financial goals, budgeting effectively, and regularly reviewing your financial progress. When you are accountable, you are less likely to make impulsive or irresponsible financial choices.

Accountable leaders and financially responsible individuals are more likely to achieve their goals and secure their financial future. By adopting this leadership principle, you can ensure that you stay on track and make informed financial decisions.

9. EMPATHY

Empathy is the ability to understand and share the feelings of others. It is a vital trait for leaders as it allows them to connect with their team on a deeper level, fostering trust and cooperation.

Empathy is a powerful tool in a leader's arsenal. Being able to understand and connect with the feelings and perspectives of others is essential. Letting people know that you have faced similar challenges and have overcome them.

When people see that you've been where they are and have risen to the top, they believe you can guide them from their current position to their desired destination. Your ability to empathize, connect emotionally, and show compassion is what creates trust and loyalty.

By being an empath, you create a network of support and trust in your financial journey. It is not just about your success but also about uplifting those you care about.

10. CONTINUOUS LEARNING

Leaders are lifelong learners. They understand that knowledge is power, and they are committed to self-improvement. They seek opportunities to acquire new skills and insights to stay at the forefront of their field.

Continuous learning means staying informed about financial trends, investment opportunities, and personal finance strategies. It involves seeking out financial education and regularly updating your financial knowledge.

Leaders who prioritize continuous learning in their financial endeavours are more likely to make informed decisions and adapt to changing financial landscapes. Your financial success is closely tied to your willingness to learn and grow.

11. CONFIDENCE

Confidence is the spark that ignites leadership. A leader's self-assuredness radiates through their actions and decisions, inspiring trust and belief in their abilities. This confidence extends to both self-belief and trust in their team.

Leaders exude confidence. They believe in themselves, their decisions, and their team. This confidence is not just self-assuredness but is also rooted in the ability to consistently deliver results. The world only bows for results.

Confidence empowers leaders to make critical choices without hesitation. It fuels the desire to take on challenges and embrace new opportunities. A confident leader encourages their team to rise to the occasion, fostering a culture of success.

By inspiring confidence through their actions, leaders motivate others to follow them. Their achievements and their unwavering belief in their team are contagious, making people want to be part of their journey.

Confidence is not solely about projecting strength; it also encompasses vulnerability. Great leaders are not afraid to admit their imperfections, and they lead by example. Your confidence is built on authenticity, a key factor in building trust and creating an environment of collaboration.

12. COURAGE

Courage is fundamental to leadership. Leaders confront fear but possess the ability to overcome it. They take risks, make tough decisions, and stand up for what is right. Leaders are courageous people. They are defenders of truth.

Courage is the cornerstone of effective leadership. It is the inner strength that propels leaders to confront challenges head-on, even in the face of fear and uncertainty. A leader's courage extends beyond personal bravery; it encompasses the audacity to make bold decisions, stand up for principles, and lead with conviction.

Leadership requires the courage to take calculated risks, as success often lies on the other side of fear. Whether it is pursuing an entrepreneurial venture, making a critical business decision, or standing up for what is right, courage is the driving force that propels leaders forward.

Courage also includes the willingness to admit mistakes and learn from them. Great leaders understand that failure is a natural part of growth and use these setbacks as stepping stones to success. By demonstrating resilience and unwavering determination, they inspire their team to push beyond their limits and achieve greatness.

13. DECISIVENESS
Leaders are decisive and do not succumb to procrastination. They understand that taking action is the antidote to procrastination. They make timely

decisions, ensuring that they maintain momentum. Their ability to make bold decisions and take swift action propels them forward.

Decisiveness is the compass that guides leadership. Leaders must make timely and informed decisions, as hesitation can lead to missed opportunities. Decisiveness is the key to maintaining momentum and moving forward.

Leaders who are decisive understand that the road to success is often under construction. They embrace uncertainty and understand that decision-making is a continuous process. Even when faced with imperfect information, they dare to act and adjust their course as needed.

Decisiveness is not about making impulsive choices but rather making informed ones. Leaders gather relevant data, seek input from their team, and consider the potential outcomes before making a decision. They are not deterred by the fear of failure, as they recognize that every decision, whether successful or not, contributes to their growth and experience.

14. PROBLEM-SOLVING

Leaders are natural problem solvers. They face

complex issues and difficult situations daily, using their analytical skills to make informed decisions. They see problems as opportunities to create solutions and make progress.

Problem equals business. In other words, solving problems is a key to success. When you address challenges, you make progress and financial gains. Problem-solving is the currency of progress. Leaders are natural problem solvers who thrive on challenges. They view problems as opportunities to innovate and create solutions that propel their organizations forward.

The ability to analyze complex issues, identify root causes, and develop effective solutions is a hallmark of leadership. Leaders approach problems with a structured mindset, breaking them down into manageable components and collaborating with their team to find solutions.

Problem-solving extends beyond finding answers—it's about fostering a problem-solving culture within an organization. Effective leaders empower their teams to tackle challenges collectively, recognizing that diversity of thought often leads to the most innovative solutions.

On the journey to financial freedom, these traits of a visionary leader are invaluable. Developing and nurturing these qualities will not only help you achieve your financial goals but also inspire others to join your mission. Vision, communication, empathy, integrity, confidence, adaptability, problem-solving, decisiveness, resilience, inspiration, accountability, and courage—all are essential for becoming the leader you were meant to be.

THE CORE VALUE OF LEADERS

Chapter Nine

"The making of a leader involves embracing challenges, learning from failures, and consistently embodying the values that inspire others to follow."
- Unknown

In my years of living on earth and growing, I have come to the realization that leaders are principled people. A leader lives by principles. A man who does not stand for something shall fall for anything. For a leader to be called a great leader and to achieve this purpose, he must have values that guide his life.

As a leader, these are core values that you build and master.

1. *They believe in promoting themselves; they don't have to be found:* effective leaders are proactive in their approach. Once they get into a business, they believe in promotion. They believe that for them to have financial freedom, they have to get attention. All the fortune follows attention. They always promote their values, ideas and products. One of the most important jobs of a leader is to always get their products in front of their customers. Instead of waiting to be discovered, they actively showcase what they have to the public.

2. Great leaders believe that financial success is never assured; but always a product of hard work and perseverance: like someone said, poor people believe in living a lottery lifestyle; but successful people believe in living an action lifestyle. Mindset is everything in life. Great leaders believe that the journey towards financial success is a product of commitment, dedication, and the ability to navigate obstacles with determination.

3. Great leaders believe in service; not in self-serving: for you to achieve financial freedom in life. You must be devoted to a life of service to humanity. If service is below you, then success is beyond you. Exceptional leaders prioritize serving others beyond pursuing their own agenda. They do not only take responsibility, they take more and more responsibilities in life. Because that's the path to growth and greatness. Their slogan is People First. Leadership is about making a positive impact.

4. Great leaders believe in doing what no one else is willing to do: they go the extra mile. The difference between great achievers of financial freedom and others is that they go the extra mile. Leaders love to live above average life. Leaders love to take on responsibilities and make tough decisions. For you to achieve financial freedom in life as a leader, you must both be tough and soft. Most leaders with this mindset are proactive problem solvers. They're unafraid to step into an uncharted territory. Leadership involves the willingness to take on responsibilities that others may want to avoid.

5. Great leaders who achieve financial freedom pay attention to connections and networks: yes, they understand the importance of building and nurturing connections and networks. They understand that relationships play a crucial role in business and personal success. By actively cultivating a strong network, these leaders create opportunities for collaboration, resource sharing, and valuable insights.

Networks open doors for partnership, mentorship and business opportunities. Great leaders understand the power of building solid relationships in achieving financial success.

6. Successful leaders who want to achieve financial freedom, don't dwell on strategies but on execution: someone said, execution is the missing link in the achievement of financial freedom in so many people's lives. While strategies are essential, the real value comes from effective implementation. Great leaders have a bias towards actions. They ensure that plans are translated into results. Ultimately, most leaders understand that success is a product of the result of effective execution of a well-thought-out strategy.

7. Great leaders who want to achieve financial freedom measure work in terms of its compounding effects: yes, they measure work in terms of the compounding effects of their efforts. Rather than merely evaluating work in isolation, they consider how each task contributes to long-term growth and financial success. They believe that consistent and high-quality efforts can lead to cumulative and amplified results. They view their work as an investment that builds upon itself.

8. Finally, they believe that the payoff is the reward of their hard work and not the motivation. Yes, leaders who achieve financial freedom in life are motivated by a deep sense of purpose rather than mere monetary gains. While they acknowledge the importance of reaping the benefits of their hard work, the primary objective stems from a genuine dedication to their vision, mission or the impact that they want to make. They view financial freedom as a byproduct of their commitment and diligence to their work. I often say that entrepreneurs work for something greater than money, which is purpose.

10

BUILDING YOUR DREAM TEAM

Chapter Ten

> "The greatest leader is not necessarily the one who does the greatest things. He is the one that gets the people to do the greatest things."
> - Ronald Reagan

You are a good leader, and that's a fact. But leadership doesn't stop there. It is a journey, and the next important step is personal development. However, it is equally essential to be deliberate when it comes to assembling your team. The Master Jesus, a profound leader in history, started his ministry by carefully handpicking his dream team. He understood that true leadership couldn't flourish without the right people by his side. He knew that if you have big dreams, you need a dream team to make them a reality.

Great leaders around the world have recognized that their leadership can only reach its full potential with the right individuals around them. As the saying goes, "The intelligence of a ruler is known by the people that surround him." To achieve your goals and make a lasting impact, you must be intentional about selecting the right team members. If you have significant aspirations, it is crucial to put together a dream team.

When I started my own business, I had to build a team of over 20,000 people that I've been leading for the past several years. This achievement was made possible by a deliberate selection process. I did not know these people from the beginning. I started by organizing seminars, realizing that I couldn't accomplish everything on my own. A leader's role is to identify and nurture talent, helping others realize their potential. To find your dream team, you must actively seek out those who can contribute to your vision.

Building a dream team begins with you taking the initiative to look for them. The Master Jesus didn't wait for his disciples to come to him. He actively sought them out and selected them for his mission. This proactive approach is a critical component of leadership.

If you want to make a significant impact in life, you must be deliberate about who you select for your team. Consider who you need on your team to achieve your goals because no one succeeds in leadership alone. Leadership is based on timeless principles. A leader can only scale his impact by empowering other leaders. To do this, you must build a dream team.

If you want to build, you can't build alone. You have to look for partners; you have to seek out inner circles. You need inner circles, a mastermind group, people you can empower, and those who empower others. This is the leadership model of the Master. He had an inner circle, consisting of John the Beloved, and another inner circle with John, Peter, and James. Then He had the twelve, the seventy, the 120, and the 520. This hierarchy is built on the level of trust and loyalty within the group. Your inner circle depends on how much trust and confidence they have in you and you have in them.

As a leader, you must study the people you surround yourself with to know who to be close to. John the Beloved, the one who is trusted the most, leads the inner circle, followed by the next inner circles, then the twelve, the seventy, the 120, and the 500. This is how leadership works.

Within my circle of influence, there has been an inner caucus among the 14 to 15 people that has developed over the past five years or more. Remember the 20/80 rule. It means that 80% of your results come from 20% of your team. Among the people surrounding you, some you can confide in more than others. The leadership journey starts with identifying yourself as a leader, developing your leadership potential, and selecting your team. You must have inner circles, a circle of influence – who are the people you need to work with? You are the one who must seek them out, don't wait for them. You have to look for them, select them, and reach out to them.

I reached out to each member of my team individually, spending various amounts of time with them on the phone to convince them that they could do it. Then, I co-opted them into the group, held regular meetings, gained their respect and confidence, and began pouring myself into them.

Leadership is not about power; it's about empowerment. The master was always teaching his disciples, often different things from what he taught others. He said to them, 'Unto you, it is given to know the secrets, but unto them, it's not.' There are principles and secrets of life that you impart to your inner circle. You try to reproduce yourself in them because you want to multiply. You want them to do what you are doing. That's how leadership scales.

After you empower them and see that they respond to your teachings and empowerment, you allow them to participate. Leadership is about participation. You start making them do what you do, putting them on stage, and giving them exposure. When I started my business, I spent almost a year on Zoom, from Sunday to Sunday, running meetings multiple times a day. Some of the leaders I selected were part of the audience and saw the way I poured myself into people.

In addition to the regular meetings, I held leadership mentor calls every month, developing slides for what they would learn. Many would have paid a significant amount for such a seminar, but I wholeheartedly shared the knowledge on Zoom. These people were blown away by my commitment to developing human capital.

Leadership is about impact. It's about being ready to burn yourself in order to give light to the world. These people saw that leadership in me and wanted to be part of something bigger than themselves. After selecting them, I allowed them to participate and created a structured system.

Since I had been training and pouring myself into them, I emphasized the importance of showing up. I told them that leadership is about showing up every day of your life. Presence equals power. Whether it's a tribal meeting, church gathering, or political event, being consistently present commands respect and opens doors for opportunities.

Even before I officially selected them, these individuals understood the importance of showing up. This commitment to presence was instilled from the beginning, as I had created the platform.

So I told all of them that they must show up all their lives if they want to make an impact. They must realize that leaders show up all their lives. And these guys kept following my instructions. They kept showing up and showing up. Then it got to a point.

I now selected them. After selecting them, the next thing is, as I told you, when a leader adds a leader to himself, it's because he wants to scale or multiply. So you must also know how to begin to put them on the stage, how to expose them.

After some time, I had leaders who took care of Monday, Tuesday, Wednesday, Thursday, Friday, Saturday, and Sunday. And guess what? Even though I started partnering with them, I pulled out completely. Then they got to a point where they could handle the call and the Zoom. And as of today, even if I do not show up to the meeting for a week, the team runs seamlessly. All of them have grown to the extent that they can conduct the Zoom meetings from the beginning to the end. That is how to scale. I have been able to scale. I have also been able to multiply, and I have been able to develop leaders that DO.

The McDonald brothers got stuck because they did not know how to scale. They did not know that to scale you have to reproduce yourself. What they were doing in one spot that attracted so many people to them could be reproduced in the same location, then another location. They were only deploying themselves in that location. They did not know that to scale, you must duplicate. In fact, one of the secrets of scaling is duplication. First, look at what works, perfect it and duplicate it. That's how the Mr. Biggs of this world was born. The Tantalizer, the KFC, the TFC, and so on.

You can scale up by duplicating your system. So I duplicated what I had perfected in others, and then they were able to do that. As an accomplished entrepreneur, you must get your business to a point where it can work without you. You have to create a system. A system is a process that produces consistent results.

If you add leaders, you multiply. If you add followers, you only add. Great leaders add leaders, good leaders add followers.

The process begins with selecting your team members. As a leader, you must recognize the potential in others and encourage them to join your mission. Remember, it is not just about what you know but also about who you know. However, do not wait for others to come to you; you must actively seek out and select your team.

In my journey of leading over 20,000 individuals, I started by organizing seminars and attracting people who resonated with my vision. I could see their potential, and I actively pursued them. I reached out, spoke with them individually, and explained my vision. Many of them didn't even realize their leadership potential until I showed them the way.

The Master Jesus had his inner circle, and he regularly met with them separately from the larger group. This principle holds true for all forms of leadership, whether in business, church, or any other field. You must create an inner circle, an inner caucus, a mastermind group, and empower those within it. This is the path to multiplying your leadership.

The inner circle should be chosen based on the level of trust and loyalty they have in you. Just like the Master had John the Beloved, the three inner circles (John, Peter, and James), the twelve, the seventy, the one hundred and twenty, and the five hundred, your team should have various levels of trust and commitment. You, as a leader, must be discerning about the individuals you bring into your inner circle, as each level of trust reflects a different level of commitment.

Even within the inner circle, there are individuals with whom you can confide more and others with whom you cannot. As a leader, you must be able to identify those who can be trusted most. In my experience, I have regularly met with a smaller group of around 14 to 15 people, building a deep sense of trust and loyalty with them over the years.

This process begins with recognizing your leadership potential, developing your skills, and then actively selecting your team. Be proactive; don't wait for your dream team to come to you. Seek them out, choose them, and reach out to them individually.

After selecting your team, it is time to empower them. Leadership is not about wielding power but about empowering others. You should teach, mentor, and pour your knowledge and experience into your team members. Just like the Master Jesus taught his disciples, you should share valuable insights, secrets, and principles that are not widely known.

Your inner circle should be a fertile ground where you replicate your leadership abilities in others. Your goal is to multiply your influence, and this starts by empowering those around you. You may find that some of your chosen team members didn't initially recognize their leadership potential. However, with your guidance, they will grow into strong leaders themselves.

Once you have empowered your team, it is time to let them participate. Leadership is about engagement and involvement. You should gradually assign them tasks and responsibilities that align with your vision. Allow them to take on leadership roles, and gradually expose them to new challenges.

In my journey, I spent a significant amount of time on Zoom, conducting seminars and pouring my knowledge into the group. I was consistent, showing up every day, and setting an example for my team. I made it clear that leaders always show up, and the power of presence cannot be underestimated. When you are consistently present and engaged, you command respect and are top of mind for opportunities and responsibilities. The game of leadership is, that monkeys do what monkeys see. People don't do what you tell them, but what you show them.

By following this process of selecting, empowering,

and allowing participation, you can build a dream team that will help you achieve your goals. Remember, leadership is about multiplying your impact by empowering others, and your dream team is an essential part of this equation.

11

THE ULTIMATE PRICE-SACRIFICE

Chapter Eleven

"Sacrifice transforms privilege into responsibility; it is the mark of true nobility."
- Marquess Sebastian

Leadership is not a position or a title; it is a choice, a commitment, and a sacrifice. You cannot get up unless you give up. For you to have the prize, you must pay the price. You must be ready to pay the price.

So, what is leadership really about?

It is the willingness to make significant sacrifices for the greater good of all. It is about putting the needs and well-being of your people above your own. Once you step into leadership, you cease to live for yourself and start living for others. It is a sacrifice, akin to putting yourself on the altar of sacrifice to bring life to others. Leaders are like candles; they burn themselves to give light to other people.

Leadership, at its core, is all about others. It is not about you. To be an effective leader, you must understand that your top priority is putting others first. Leaders prioritize the well-being, welfare, and development of those they lead. They dedicate their lives to their team and are always with their followers, just as Jesus was always with his disciples. Leadership is not about power; it is about empowerment. It is about living your life for other people's success, helping them succeed, and being selfless. The moment you step into leadership, you must have a heart for the people and be a lover of the people. You will sacrifice your own life to see others succeed.

A wise man once wisely said, "We rise by lifting other people." Zig Ziglar echoed a similar sentiment, "You will have to find whatever you want in life when you help enough find what you want in life." Richard Branson also understood that success is making other people's lives better, and leadership aligns with this principle of making other people's lives better.

Leaders do not play it safe; they embrace discomfort. Instead of staying outside the box, leaders break the box and reside perpetually in the discomfort zone. To be effective in leadership, you must be willing to give up your personal gains, whether they are financial rewards, recognition, or comfort. The higher you ascend in leadership, the more you must give up your rights and privileges for the benefit of all.

Personal sacrifice is a hallmark of great leaders. They know that leadership requires them to take on stress, emotional burdens, and the problems of those they lead. It is not just a figurehead position; it is a hands-on role. By risking personal gain and comfort, leaders inspire others to do the same, pushing them to be better and achieve more than they ever thought possible.

Leaders understand the concept of the emotional bank account. You must invest in people if you want to withdraw trust, loyalty, and commitment. When you deposit positivity, support, and guidance into the lives of your team members, they will reciprocate. They will want to do good for you because you have helped them succeed. Leadership is about raising people, making them better, and guiding them towards their full potential. It is about making them who you are, bringing them to your level, or even beyond.

You must not shy away from tough decisions; embrace them. Make decisions, defend them, and take both the credit and the blame. Do not pass the blame onto others when things go wrong, as many do. Leaders are strong and unapologetic in their decision-making, which garners respect, even if not everyone agrees with every choice they make.

Great leaders understand that leadership is not always about popularity; it involves doing what is necessary for the greater good. They are willing to make tough decisions that may be criticized initially, knowing that these choices are necessary for long-term success. They take on the responsibility of these decisions, facing criticism, but ultimately reaping the rewards of their boldness.

Leaders lead by example. The first person they lead is themselves, and people follow leaders who practice what they preach. Actions speak louder than words. Leaders' actions serve as models for their team's behaviour and attitude. Therefore, leaders must constantly demonstrate their commitment, dedication, work ethic, and results. People naturally follow leaders who are stronger than themselves.

By setting an example, leaders inspire their teams to emulate their values and work ethic. It is a leader's actions that people follow, not just their words. Leadership is about being a copycat, but you must copy the right "cat." People do what they see leaders do, and a leader's behaviour serves as a model for their team's actions.

Leaders often make personal sacrifices for the greater good. Some even pay the ultimate price. Think of leaders like Indira Gandhi, Martin Luther King, Nelson Mandela, and even Jesus Christ. Sacrificing for the benefit of others is an integral part of leadership. Leaders are not fearful; they are not self-serving. They willingly step into the line of fire, facing life-threatening situations, for the sake of their mission.

A great leader knows that facing danger is part of

the job description. You need to understand the price you need to pay to achieve your vision, which often includes sacrificing your well-being. Leadership is not about enjoying the perks; it involves bearing the weight of responsibility and making the hard choices.

To be a great leader, you should not just have a vision; you must have a big vision. Achieving long-term goals demands significant sacrifice of time, energy, and resources. Leaders invest in their vision, working tirelessly to bring it to fruition. Understand that instant gratification is not the goal; building something enduring that will benefit others for years to come is the goal.

Leaders build trust and loyalty over time through selfless actions. Relationships are not formed instantly; they are forged through time and consistency. Leaders must earn respect and trust capital, which enables them to guide their teams effectively. It is a long and ongoing process of demonstrating your commitment and dedication to the team's success.

Great leaders inspire and motivate their teams to achieve what they once thought impossible. Inspiring others is a great sacrifice in itself. It takes dedication, commitment, and a strong belief in the potential of those you lead. Fostering a culture of excellence and encouraging people to dream bigger and achieve more is a goal that is always on the mind of the leader.

A leader demonstrates a high level of resilience and endurance. They persevere through the most challenging times, maintaining their energy and determination. Leaders do not doubt, and they do not fear, because doing so would erode the confidence of their followers. Leaders stand strong, knowing that their unwavering commitment will lead their teams to success.

Leadership is not a path for the faint of heart; it is a journey of sacrifice, commitment, and unwavering dedication to the greater good. It requires you to put others first, take responsibility for difficult decisions, and lead by example. It involves personal sacrifice, resilience, and endurance.

As a leader, you must understand that your role is

not about power but empowerment. It is not about selfishness but selflessness. You must lead with the vision of creating a better future and building trust and loyalty through your actions. Leaders inspire, motivate, and persevere, paving the way for others to succeed.

Leadership is a path of sacrifice and a path of profound impact. Strive to make the world better by helping others become the best versions of themselves. Sacrifice is at the core of leadership, and it is a choice that great leaders make every day.

12.

THE POWER OF GRATITUDE

Chapter Twelve

> "Gratitude is the inward feeling of kindness received. Thankfulness is the natural impulse to express that feeling. Thanksgiving is the following of that impulse."
> - Henry Van Dyke

Gratitude is the source of all abundance. You might be wondering why I chose to begin with this statement. To express leadership effectively, you need to maintain certain perspectives, beliefs, fundamentals, and values. Gratitude is at the core of these principles. Gratitude is not just a simple emotion; it is a powerful force that can attract wealth, prosperity, and abundance into your life. It is like a magnet that draws in all the good things you desire.

Gratitude is a profound emotion. It requires you to be thankful, appreciate the positives in life, and maintain a positive outlook. Successful leaders possess this quality. As they embark on their leadership journey and pursue growth, they do so with a deep sense of gratitude.

I have often mentioned that leaders are enthusiastic, happy, excited, and full of energy. Now, you might be wondering, "What's their secret to maintaining such high energy levels and enthusiasm?" The answer is simple: gratitude. Gratitude is the fuel that keeps their fire burning.

Happiness and gratitude go hand in hand. It is almost impossible to be unhappy when you're grateful. I have observed that the unhappiest people in the world are the ungrateful ones. You cannot maintain a state of gratitude and be unhappy simultaneously. It is just not possible.

Successful leaders are always mindful and grateful for everything bad or good things, big or small, that happen in their lives. They appreciate their life experiences and are grateful to the Divine. They practice gratitude consistently. This practice attracts good health, wealth, strength, happiness, better relationships, and overall well-being into their lives. Moreover, it enables them to surround themselves with the right people and stay in control of their circumstances.

Gratitude is all about focusing on what you have left, not what you have lost. Ungrateful people tend to dwell on their losses rather than acknowledge what they still have. Some people may have almost everything they need in life, but if they are fixated on that one thing they lack, they become unhappy. They blame God, themselves, and those around them, and sadness takes over. But if they were to take a step back and look at their lives, they would see a picture of blessing and abundance. That is the power of shifting perspective. People who fall into this category must make a paradigm shift in their lives. Because it is practising gratitude consistently by focusing more on what they already have, will eventually bring that one thing that they lack, which they're looking for in their lives.

If you want to attract abundance into your life—good health, wealth, strength, and everything you desire—you must cultivate an attitude of gratitude. It is not just a nice-to-have; it is the only way to ascend to new heights. Gratitude is the source of all abundance, the gateway to your altitude.

By maintaining an attitude of gratitude, you open yourself up to the limitless possibilities the universe has to offer. It is a mindset that can change your life and propel you toward financial freedom.
Gratitude is a powerful force that can transform your leadership and financial journey. By understanding its significance and practising it in your life, you can open doors to abundance, success, and happiness.

As you conclude this chapter, I want to express my gratitude to you, the reader, for embarking on this journey with me. I am thankful for your attention and commitment to learning about leadership for financial freedom. Your willingness to explore these concepts will not only benefit your life but the lives you touch. Always remember that leadership is a skill that everyone can learn, regardless of age or generation.

THE EMOTION OF LOVE
Another important aspect of leadership which is equally more important for a leader to practice which my mentor told me about is, the emotion of love.

When I began to practice this in my life, it changed the trajectory of my entire destiny. I would like to mention it in this chapter.

Practising emotions of love involves cultivating a mindset that expresses care, compassion and understanding towards oneself and others. It includes acts of kindness, empathy, and fostering positive connections. Ultimately, it's about nurturing meaningful relationships and contributing to a more supportive environment.

My mentor told me you must never say anything negative about anything or anyone. You must never speak negatively about the place you have worked in before or the people you have worked with before. Which is a common practice for many people. He told me that eeeeeeattitude is anti-success. Making mony is learning how to gt it without infringing on the rights of others. If you keep displaying such an attitude in your life, you are pushing success away from yourself.

So how do you achieve financial freedom by practicing the emotions of love? Here are some ways to implement it:

1. Empathy: You must understand the feelings of your team and actively listen to their concerns and challenges.

2. Supportive Environment: You have to constantly support their work. Leaders work for the people who work for them. With that team members feel valued, respected and willing to always express themselves.

3. Recognition And Appreciation: It is very important to always show recognition and appreciation to your team members. Regularly express gratitude for individuals' efforts and contributions to the growth of the team. By that, you build strong trust capital with your team members.

4. Develop Relationships: You have to invest time in your team members. I sometimes go out of my way by calling them and spending quality time with them on the phone. By this, you build strong relationships and get to know them on a one-on-one basis. And it demonstrates that you really have a genuine interest in them.

5. Effective Communication: You have to communicate with transparency and integrity. Openness brings a kind of trust from your team members. People only want you to do business with the people that they know, trust and like. Keep your team informed about relevant matters and encourage dialogue.

6. Conflict Resolution: Your ability to handle difficult conflicts that may arise from your team, will stand you out as an effective leader. Remember, what you don't confront, you don't conquer. To achieve financial freedom, you must be bold and courageous. You must learn how to handle conflicts with a compassionate approach.

7. Coaching And Personal Development: Like I said before, you must pour yourself into your team, if you want to achieve financial freedom. Apart from regular meetings that I often have with my team. I also create a monthly leadership mentor call. The way to get us to give. If you don't deposit in their emotional bank account, you cannot withdraw.

8. Lead By Example: Be the leader you want to see in your team. Be the change that you want to see in the world if you want to achieve financial freedom in your life. As you have been told earlier, leadership is a game of being a copycat. But people must copy the right cat. So you must show integrity, kindness and collaboration consistently in your team.

9. *Flexibility And Understanding:* For you to achieve financial freedom, you must recognize individuals' needs and concerns. You must understand life and work balance in your team. You must show understanding among your members.

10. *Celebrating Success:* You just celebrate achievements, both small and big. Create a culture of celebrating milestones achievements and celebrating successes, and constantly create a positive energy in your team.

Will you like to meet my Hero, my Champion, my Coach, my Role Model, the man who is behind the making of Pst Mike? Will you like to be like me? Will you like to achieve financial freedom in life?

He is always ready to meet with you. He made my life so beautiful and I know He can also make yours beautiful as well. He said, *"Follow me and I will make you…"* He is the maker of destiny. He shaped my life. To achieve greatness in life you need to give your life to Jesus. That was the decision I made that changed my entire life.

Say, Lord Jesus, I'm sorry for my sins. I want you to come into my life. I reject satan and all his evil works. I promise not to go back into my sin. I declare that I'm now born again. Praise God! You are welcome to the family of success. You have come into abundant life. Congratulations!

Note: Unless you change who you are. You can never have what you want. Life does not give you what you want.

Life gives you what you are. Your identity is the gateway to
your prosperity. See you at the top!

About the author

Michael Onalaja is a pastor, international inspirational speaker, #1 best-selling author, financial advisor, mentor of mentors, leaders of leaders, businessmen, and entrepreneur.

He is a member of the Institute of Chartered Accountants of Nigeria. He was an employee with Dunlop Nigeria Plc for 10 years before he resigned to pursue his life's dream of financial freedom, entrepreneurship, and leadership. He has since then been a keynote speaker at national and international events, making an impact and transforming lives with his knowledge.

He is married to Olayinka Omosebi Onalaja and their union are blessed with children. His personal vision for life is to elevate the financial well-being of people, develop entrepreneurs and improve the standard of living of humanity.